W9-ASC-732

Birthright Citizenship

Toney Allman

ReferencePoint
Press

San Diego, CA

© 2020 ReferencePoint Press, Inc.
Printed in the United States

For more information, contact:
ReferencePoint Press, Inc.
PO Box 27779
San Diego, CA 92198
www.ReferencePointPress.com

LIBRARY OF CONGRESS CATALOGING-IN-PUBLICATION DATA

Names: Allman, Toney, author.
Title: Birthright Citizenship/Toney Allman.
Description: San Diego, CA: ReferencePoint Press, Inc. 2020. | Series:
  Immigration Issues | Includes bibliographical references and index.
Identifiers: LCCN 2019035547 (print) | LCCN 2019035548 (ebook) | ISBN
  9781682827635 (library binding) | ISBN 9781682827642 (ebook)
Subjects: LCSH: Citizenship—United States—Juvenile literature.
Classification: LCC KF4704 .A949 2020 (print) | LCC KF4704 (ebook) | DDC
  342.7308/3—dc23
LC record available at https://lccn.loc.gov/2019035547
LC ebook record available at https://lccn.loc.gov/2019035548

Contents

Citizens at Birth

In October 2018, President Donald Trump revealed in a television interview that he planned to end birthright citizenship. Trump stated, "We're the only country in the world where a person comes in and has a baby, and the baby is essentially a citizen of the United States . . . with all of those benefits. It's ridiculous. It's ridiculous. And it has to end."[1] Critics were quick to point out that more than thirty countries offer birthright citizenship—but the United States and Canada are the only two developed nations to offer it. In the United States, birthright citizenship is a constitutional guarantee that any child born on US soil is an American citizen.

An Unconstitutional Plan?

Many who heard Trump's pronouncement worried that he was proposing the reversal of a long-standing US policy on citizenship, one guaranteed by the Fourteenth Amendment. In addition, it seemed that Trump was suggesting that the president could alter the constitutional guarantee without an act of Congress. The citizenship clause of the Fourteenth Amendment states, "All persons born or naturalized in the United States, and subject to the jurisdiction thereof, are citizens of the United States and of the State wherein they reside." Legal rulings have interpreted that wording to mean that anyone born on US soil is a citizen. (The few exceptions to this policy include children born to foreign diplomats or children of enemy soldiers temporarily housed on US soil.) Members of Congress, for the most part, disputed the president's proposal. Representative Mike Coffman of Colorado, for instance, remarked, "I hate to break the news to President Trump, but the Supreme Court isn't going to let him rewrite immigration law by executive [order], nor should they."[2] Paul D. Ryan, the Speaker of the House at the time, asserted, "Well, you obviously cannot do that. You cannot end birthright citizenship with an executive order."[3]

Immigration attorney Raul A. Reyes was more vociferous in his criticism, calling the proposal "callous and dangerous," insisting that the concept of birthright citizenship "is not ridiculous at all." Furthermore, he insisted that no president could change birthright citizenship policy simply by issuing an order to do so:

> An executive order targeting birthright citizenship would be blatantly unconstitutional and go against over 100 years of legal precedent. . . . The only way to lawfully change birthright citizenship is through a constitutional amendment, requiring the approval of two-thirds of both chambers of Congress and ratification by three-fourths of the states; a constitutional convention; or if the Supreme Court decides upon a radical reinterpretation of the issue.[4]

Support for Limiting Birthright Citizenship

Despite the critics, the president's idea finds support among those who believe that the wording of the Fourteenth Amendment has long been misinterpreted because it does not explicitly bestow citizenship in all circumstances. In addition, a few argue that a limitation on birthright citizenship is not unconstitutional and may be within the president's authority. Michael Anton, a former official of the National Security Council and lecturer and researcher at Hillsdale College in Michigan, writes, "An executive order could specify to federal agencies that the children of noncitizens are not citizens. Such an order would, of course, immediately be challenged in the courts. But officers in all three branches of government—the president no less than judges—take similar oaths to defend the Constitution. Why shouldn't the president act to defend the clear meaning of the 14th Amendment?"[5]

Anton recognizes that any executive order limiting birthright citizenship would be subject to a decision by the Supreme Court, but he and some others welcome such a legal challenge. They argue that the Fourteenth Amendment was never meant to allow anyone at all to enter the country in order to give birth to a citizen. They believe that the court system would logically have no choice but to uphold the president's or Congress's right to clarify the conditions under which a person born on US soil is a citizen.

In 2018 and again in 2019, President Donald Trump commented publicly that he wanted to end birthright citizenship. Birthright citizenship is a constitutional guarantee that any child born on US soil is an American citizen.

A Divisive Issue

As of the fall of 2019, President Trump had not moved to end unrestricted birthright citizenship, although while speaking to reporters in August 2019 he reiterated his serious desire to do so. Thus, the arguments still rage about whether this should be done. Many view the president's statements as part of a larger political conflict over US immigration policy; however, as a distinct issue, proponents fight to restrict the citizenship clause while critics deny the ease at which this could be accomplished. Bound up in these arguments are the legality of such an action, the meaning of the Constitution, and the pros and cons of maintaining the policy of granting citizenship to anyone born in the United States.

"Why shouldn't the president act to defend the clear meaning of the 14th Amendment?"[5]

—Michael Anton, political lecturer

Chapter One

The History of Birthright Citizenship

The debate that began with President Trump's comments is not the first time that birthright citizenship has been the subject of a controversy. The intention and meaning of the Fourteenth Amendment has been debated since its ratification. The Fourteenth Amendment is not one of the original amendments to the Constitution adopted in 1791. It was ratified in 1868, in the wake of the US Civil War.

The Original Constitution and Citizenship

The Constitution does not even define citizenship, although it does refer to citizenship in regard to who is eligible for elected office. Article II states that only natural-born citizens or those who were citizens at the time the Constitution was adopted are eligible to be president of the United States. Other than that, the Constitution refers only to "persons," "person," or "people" to indicate Americans bound by its laws. There is also no mention of race, gender, or economic status in referencing the people of the United States. Nevertheless, most scholars are certain that the Constitution's framers had a clear idea of what they meant by the word *citizen*: white male landowners. Before she became a Supreme Court justice, Ruth Bader Ginsburg wrote, "Indeed, it left out the majority of the adult population: slaves, debtors, paupers, Indians, and women. As framed in 1787, the Constitution was a document of governance for and by white, propertied adult males—a document for people who were free from dependence on others and therefore not susceptible to influence or control by masters, overlords, or superiors."[6]

Historian Mary Beth Norton says that it never occurred to the framers of the Constitution to define *citizen* because of the European society from which they came. In that world, everyone knew what a citizen was. In the eighteenth century, and long before, Norton says, people did not think in terms of individuals but in terms of households. She explains, "Each household had a male head, who controlled the household's property, directed its activities, fulfilled its obligations to the community through militia service or political participation, and was regarded by the law as the ruler of his own 'little commonwealth.'"[7] Women, minor children, servants, and slaves were dependent on the male head of the household and were not politically significant. That free, independent, male individual was the assumed citizen, with all the rights and obligations provided by the Constitution. Wives and children derived their citizenship (albeit without all the rights of a citizen) through the husband and father.

In addition, citizenship was presumably determined by birth. The founding fathers brought with them the English common law concept that if one were born on British soil, then one was a British subject of the king. This principle is known as jus soli, meaning "right of the soil." This principle would have logically carried over to the new country, too. People born on American soil were American citizens and subject to US law.

Congress Weighs In

Less than two years after the Constitution was ratified in 1788, however, Congress recognized that jus soli was inadequate as a definition of citizenship. In March 1790, Congress passed "An act to establish an uniform Rule of Naturalization," which laid out who was or could become a citizen; basically, white people.

Although not a part of the Constitution, this Naturalization Act defined citizenship for the first time and added to the principle of jus soli. First, the law established citizenship to be hereditary. In other words, children born to American fathers while the family was abroad were deemed American citizens, even though they were not born in the United States. This principle is known by the Latin phrase jus sanguinis, or the "right of the blood." It ensured that children born to diplomats or others living abroad were citizens, just as their fathers were, and that the sons would be allowed to vote and own property once they were adults.

The 1790 Naturalization Act also defined how immigrants to the United States could become fully naturalized citizens with the right to vote. It says, in part, that "any Alien [noncitizen] being a free white person, who shall have resided within . . . the United States for the term of two years, may be admitted to become a citizen."[8] It further requires that such immigrants be of good character and swear an oath to the Constitution, and

At the time of the signing of the Constitution (pictured), no one would have thought to define who is or is not a citizen. Citizenship was determined by birth and was a privilege extended only to white male landowners.

it specifies that once a man has become a citizen, all of his children are citizens, too. Although the 1790 act was modified several times during the next few years, its general principles remained the law of the land for decades. The exclusion of Native Americans, African slaves, and other people of color persisted.

The Importance of Jus Soli

As time passed, the issue of citizenship and its qualifications was also addressed in the courts. In a landmark case in 1844, the principles of jus soli and jus sanguinis were weighed, and birthright citizenship won out. The court case involved a woman named Julia Lynch and her status as a US citizen. In 1815, Julia's Irish parents had come to New York to join her father's brother, Thomas Lynch, for an extended stay. During their stay, Julia was born. Julia's family later returned home to Ireland. When Julia was grown, her uncle Thomas died, leaving behind valuable New York real estate. At that time, no one could inherit property in the United States who was not an American citizen. Julia Lynch claimed the right of inheritance as a citizen because she had been born in the United States. Her uncle's business partner and another brother filed suit against her, claiming that she was a British subject because her father was a British subject, thus invoking jus sanguinis. Her father had been only a temporary immigrant to the United States and had never expressed a desire to apply for citizenship.

Judge Lewis H. Sandford of New York's Court of Chancery ruled, however, that Julia Lynch was a citizen of the United States by right of birth (jus soli). In a lengthy decision, he stated, among other things, that although the Constitution was silent on the definition of citizenship, it had defined eligibility for the presidency using the phrase "natural born citizen," and thus he treated the question of whether the candidate's parents might be "aliens" as irrelevant. In addition, Sandford asserted that citizenship was a national right bestowed by the Constitution and not by individual states. Sandford concluded, "Upon principle, therefore, I can entertain no doubt, but that by the law of the United States, every person born within the dominions and allegiance of the United States, whatever were the situation of his parents, is a natural born citizen."[9]

The *Dred Scott* Decision

The judge's ruling seemed to confirm the principle of birthright citizenship, but it was not the law of the land. In the highly controversial *Dred Scott* decision of 1857, the Supreme Court ignored and even contradicted this principle. Dred Scott was born into slavery in Virginia around 1795. During his lifetime, he lived in several states, including Missouri, Illinois, and Minnesota, with his owners. At that time, the United States was composed of free states, where slavery was illegal, and slaveholding states, where it was accepted. When Scott's last owner died in Missouri (a slave state), the owner's widow turned the estate over to her brother and returned east. Scott then sued in the courts for his freedom and that of his wife and children, claiming that the time he had lived in the free states of Minnesota and Illinois made him a free man. For eleven years, the case made its way through the court system as rulings were appealed, until the suit was heard by the US Supreme Court. On March 6, 1857, the Supreme Court ruled 7–2 against Scott.

Chief Justice Roger Taney wrote for the majority opinion, "The question is simply this: Can a Negro, whose ancestors were imported into this country, and sold as slaves, become a member of the political community formed and brought into existence by the Constitution of the United States, and as such become entitled to all the rights, and privileges, and immunities, guarantied (sic) by that instrument to the citizen?" Taney's answer was that slaves were not US citizens and never could be. He ruled that because of his race, Scott was not eligible for citizenship and indeed was a member of an "inferior class of beings"[10] to whom the Constitution did not apply. African Americans had no rights or privileges under the Constitution. They were considered property. Therefore, Scott had no standing; that is, he had no right to sue for anything and thus would remain a slave.

Outraged Reaction

The Supreme Court decision sparked immediate outrage among abolitionists (those fighting to abolish slavery). In his dissenting opinion, Justice Benjamin Curtis angrily wrote that citizenship was acquired by birth and pointed out that black people had been citizens and had voted during the ratification of the original Constitution. He argued that it was "not true, in point of fact, that the Constitution was made exclusively by the white race." And he asserted that African Americans were "in every sense part of the people of the United States."[11]

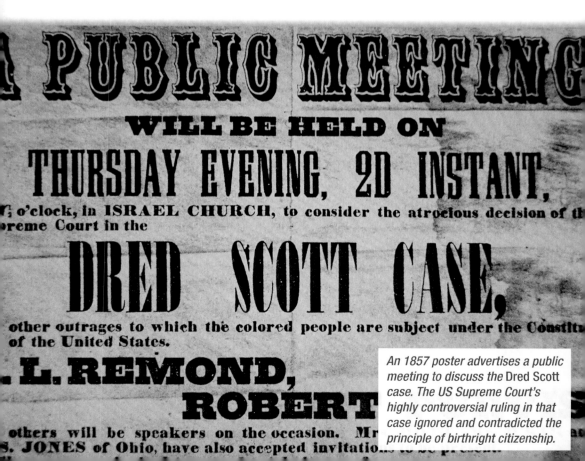

An 1857 poster advertises a public meeting to discuss the Dred Scott case. The US Supreme Court's highly controversial ruling in that case ignored and contradicted the principle of birthright citizenship.

Abraham Lincoln, a rising star in the newly formed Republican Party, publicly denounced the ruling. Senator Charles Sumner of Massachusetts vowed, "I declare that the opinion of the chief justice in the case of Dred Scott was more thoroughly abominable than anything of the kind in the history of courts. Judicial baseness reached its lowest point on that occasion."[12] Many historians today believe that the *Dred Scott* decision hastened the outbreak of the Civil War between the North and the South. It eventually resulted in President Lincoln's Emancipation Proclamation on January 1, 1863, which declared all slaves in the Confederacy to be free.

Birthrights for African Americans

After the Civil War ended in 1865 with the Confederacy's defeat, the US Congress passed the Civil Rights Act of 1866 to further protect newly freed slaves. It was the first law to define birthright citizenship. The law read, in part, "Be it enacted by the Senate and House of Representatives of the United States of America in Congress assembled, That all persons born in the United States

What Happened to Dred Scott?

After the *Dred Scott* Supreme Court decision, Scott's last owner's widow did not want to deal with owning such a controversial slave. She had remarried, and her new husband, Dr. Calvin Clifford Chaffee, was against slavery. Her brother, John F.A. Sanford, to whom she had given control of her affairs and property, died soon after the decision. The family of Scott's original Virginia owners, brothers Henry and Taylor Blow, believed that he deserved his freedom. They had provided the financial and legal help that made it possible for Scott to sue during all the years it took for the case to come before the Supreme Court. The widow, now Mrs. Chaffee, transferred Scott's ownership to Taylor Blow, who was then living in Missouri. Blow promptly emancipated Scott in court on May 26, 1857. Sadly, Scott did not have long to live in freedom. He worked as a free man in a hotel in St. Louis for about a year before dying of tuberculosis on September 17, 1858.

and not subject to any foreign power, excluding Indians not taxed, are hereby declared to be citizens of the United States."[13] (Native Americans were excluded to preserve their status as separate tribal entities with sovereign rights not subject to US law.)

Subsequently, aware that future Congresses might overturn the law and determined to reverse the damage caused by the *Dred Scott* decision, some legislators proposed and drafted the Fourteenth Amendment to the Constitution in 1866. Section 1, known as the citizenship clause, reads:

> All persons born or naturalized in the United States, and subject to the jurisdiction thereof, are citizens of the United States and of the State wherein they reside. No State shall make or enforce any law which shall abridge the privileges or immunities of citizens of the United States; nor shall any State deprive any person of life, liberty, or property, without due process of law; nor deny to any person within its jurisdiction the equal protection of the laws.[14]

Debating the Fourteenth Amendment

The section ensured that any African Americans born on US soil, whether former slaves or not, were citizens by national law and fully equal to every other citizen. Many in Congress believed that the individual states, not the federal government, should make decisions about citizens' rights. These legislators therefore engaged in vigorous debate against the amendment, seeing its passage as a route to tyranny by a government with unlimited power. Even some legislators who supported the abolition of slavery thought that the amendment went too far, especially in its assertion that every citizen had equal rights and privileges. New Jersey representative Andrew Rogers argued, "The right to vote is a privilege. The right to marry is a privilege. The right to contract is a privilege. The right to be a juror is a privilege. The right to be a judge or President of the United States is a privilege. I hold if

[Section 1] ever becomes a part of the fundamental law of the land it will prevent any state from refusing to allow anything to anybody embraced under this term of privileges and immunities."[15]

Other legislators, however, saw the amendment as necessary to protect the rights of African American citizens, especially those in the states of the former Confederacy. Representative Thaddeus Stevens of Pennsylvania argued, "[Section 1] allows Congress to correct the unjust legislation of the states, so far that the law which operates upon one man shall operate equally upon all. Whatever law punishes a white man for a crime shall punish the black man precisely in the same way and to the same degree. Whatever law protects the white man shall afford 'equal protection' to the black man."[16] Indeed, Vermont senator

"I hold if [the citizenship clause] ever becomes a part of the fundamental law of the land it will prevent any state from refusing to allow anything to anybody embraced under this term of privileges and immunities."[15]

—Andrew Rogers, New Jersey representative

In Support of the Fourteenth Amendment

Senator Jacob Howard, the lead author of the Fourteenth Amendment, argued on the Senate floor in favor of its passage:

> This amendment which I have offered is simply declaratory of what I regard as the law of the land already, that every person born within the limits of the United States, and subject to their jurisdiction, is by virtue of natural law and national law a citizen of the United States. This will not, of course, include persons born in the United States who are foreigners, aliens, who belong to the families of ambassadors or foreign ministers accredited to the Government of the United States, but will include every other class of persons.

Quoted in Craig Bannister, "Author of 14th Amendment: 'Removes All Doubt as to What Persons Are or Are Not Citizens,'" CNS News, October 31, 2018. www.cnsnews.com.

Luke Poland saw the amendment as a benefit to all Americans, including southern ones. He commented, "All causes of discord between North and South being over, we shall become a homogenous nation of freemen, dwelling together in peace and unity."[17] Despite such assurances, several of the southern states began passing laws that limited the rights of the newly freed slaves.

Ratified

In June 1866, the Senate passed the Fourteenth Amendment by a vote of 33 to 11. The House of Representatives passed it by a vote of 120 to 32. President Andrew Johnson (who opposed the amendment) sent it to the individual states for ratification later that same month. Of the thirty-seven states, twenty-eight had to ratify the amendment before it became part of the Constitution. Many states ratified it immediately, but there was some resistance. Almost all the former Confederate states refused to ratify it, but the legislators known as the Radical Republicans had a veto-proof

With the ratification of the Fourteenth Amendment in 1868, citizenship by birth became the law of the land. Babies born on US soil, regardless of their parents' nationality, are considered American citizens.

majority in Congress. They disbanded some state governments and imposed military rule on these states. Then, they passed laws requiring southern states to ratify the Fourteenth Amendment before they could regain representation in Congress. Louisiana and South Carolina became the last two states to do so. Their consent was needed in order to reach the number of states that were required to validate the change to the Constitution. The Fourteenth Amendment was finally ratified on July 9, 1868.

Guaranteed Birthright Citizenship

The Fourteenth Amendment became a part of the Constitution, and citizenship by birth—both in the country as a whole and in each individual state—was enshrined therein: "All persons born or naturalized in the United States, and subject to the jurisdiction thereof, are citizens of the United States and of the State wherein they reside." This is the basis for birthright citizenship, a concept that professor of constitutional law Garrett Epps calls "the linchpin of the current constitutional system."[18] It ensures equal citizenship for all.

Chapter Two

Interpreting the Fourteenth Amendment

Since its ratification, the Fourteenth Amendment has bestowed citizenship on millions of people, not only former slaves but also those born to immigrant or noncitizen parents. Whether the amendment should confer citizenship so easily, however, has been debated for decades. Its purpose and scope have been argued legislatively and in the courts whenever the issue of birthright citizenship arises.

What Jurisdiction Means

The wording of the citizenship clause—"All persons born or naturalized in the United States, and subject to the jurisdiction thereof, are citizens of the United States and of the State wherein they reside"—has been the focus of much of the debate concerning citizenship. Critics argue that "subject to the jurisdiction thereof" is an ambiguous phrase and open to interpretation. The term *jurisdiction* can refer to a government or to the courts, but in general it refers to the power or authority to administer justice. Law professor Garrett Epps interprets it as saying that the government has jurisdiction over everyone in the country because anyone in the country—citizen or visitor—has to obey the country's laws. He explains, "Foreign citizens are 'subject to the jurisdiction' of our police and courts when they are in the U.S., whether as tourists, legal residents, or undocumented immigrants. Only one group is not 'subject to the jurisdiction'—accredited foreign diplomats and their families, who can be expelled by the federal government but not arrested or tried." Therefore, Epps argues, the Fourteenth Amendment "means what it says."[19] In other words, anyone born in the United States has birthright citizenship, no matter who his or her parents are, where they came from, or whether they are citizens.

Though Epps sees no controversy regarding the wording of the citizenship clause, some people debate whether the amendment is really meant to apply to *anyone* born on US soil other than children of diplomats. After all, it was originally written to protect former slaves. Epps dismisses these arguments, however, stating that "over and over in the Fourteenth Amendment debates, the framers of the amendment made clear that there would be no other exclusions from the clause. Children of immigrants? They were citizens."[20]

An Alternative Meaning

Not all legal scholars agree with Epps about what *jurisdiction* means in the amendment. Some interpret the term to imply allegiance to the United States and that the country accepts this allegiance. Legal scholar John C. Eastman of Chapman University in California argues that *jurisdiction* had two meanings at the time the Fourteenth Amendment was written:

> There was what we call partial or territorial jurisdiction, that's what we equate with subject to our laws, and there was more complete or political jurisdiction to the extent that you owed allegiance to the country. And let me put it kind of in modern terms. Suppose a British citizen is here visiting as a tourist. While within our borders he is subject to our laws; he drives on the right side of the road instead

of the left or he is going to get a ticket because that's what our law says. But he is not subject to the more complete political jurisdiction. We don't call him for jury service or military service. We don't prosecute him for treason if he takes up arms against us. He is not subject to that more complete political jurisdiction just by virtue of his presence here.[21]

Eastman says that the framers of the Fourteenth Amendment made it clear during their debates that they meant what he calls "complete jurisdiction" when they wrote "subject to the jurisdiction thereof." They were referring to people who did not owe loyalty to any other country and were not subjects of another sovereign power. They were people from whom the United States expected allegiance. Indeed, Senator Lyman Trumbull argued at the time of

The shadow of deportation to Mexico was hanging over Jose and Maria Aguilar of National City, California. Complicating their situation, their two children—both born in the United States—are US citizens.

the initial debates in 1866 that "subject to the jurisdiction means subject to its complete jurisdiction, not owing allegiance to anybody else."[22] Thus, *jurisdiction* means the allegiance to and the consent of the US government. Therefore, concludes Eastman, only children born on US soil to parents who do not owe allegiance to another country should be considered US citizens by birth.

If Eastman and others like him are correct, then they have a good argument for the legal right to restrict birthright citizenship in some circumstances. Children born to people living in the United States legally and permanently would have the right to birthright citizenship because the parents are in America by the consent of the government and therefore owe allegiance only to the United States. They are subject to the "complete jurisdiction" of the country. Children born to people in the United States as legal visitors or without proper documentation (thus without the consent

An Unsung Hero

Few people, except perhaps historians, are aware of the historical importance of Wong Kim Ark. One day in 1998, Alice Wong was researching her family history and phoned the National Archives and Records Administration in San Bruno, California, to see whether it had any records about her great-grandfather, Wong Kim Ark. She knew nothing about him, but she made an appointment to visit and look over the archives. The twenty-year-old Chinese American was stunned by the reception she got when she arrived. The staff was thrilled to meet her. To her befuddled surprise, she was taken around and introduced to the whole staff as Wong Kim Ark's great-granddaughter. One archivist even asked for her autograph. Alice had no idea that her ancestor had changed immigration laws forever or that millions of Asian Americans owe their citizenship to him. She learned her proud family history that day. A college student at the time, Alice Wong was inspired to enroll in an Asian American studies class and even wrote a report about her great-grandfather and the Chinese Exclusion Acts that he successfully overcame through his lawsuit.

of the government) would not be birthright citizens. Instead, they would be citizens of the country from which their parents came and to which the parents still owed allegiance. Eastman asserts, "The issue is whether people who are just here on a short-term temporary visitor visa or not here lawfully at all are able to demand membership in the body politic without our consent."[23]

Expanding Birthright Citizenship Rights

The issue cited by Eastman is a critical one when it comes to the matter of immigration and birthright citizenship. Those concerned about illegal immigration could argue that any children born to illegal immigrants are not entitled to citizenship, and those concerned about the meaning of the Fourteenth Amendment could insist on stricter standards for bestowing birthright citizenship. Since 1868, however, when the Fourteenth Amendment became a part of the Constitution, legislative and judicial decisions have expanded rather than restricted the meaning of birthright citizenship.

Native Americans, one might argue, are certainly born within the United States, but their citizenship was not granted until 1924, when Congress passed the Indian Citizenship Act. It reads, in part, that "all noncitizen Indians born within the territorial limits of the United States be, and they are hereby, declared to be citizens of the United States: Provided that the granting of such citizenship shall not in any manner impair or otherwise affect the right of any Indian to tribal or other property."[24] Before this law was enacted, Native Americans living on tribal reservations were considered to be under the complete jurisdiction of their tribal nations, and their reservation land was their own. They were not taxed or required to obey US laws. If they left the reservation and committed a crime on US soil, they could not be arrested and tried in US courts. They were referred to tribal authorities for punishment instead. At the same time, they were not allowed to vote and had few civil rights. This situation changed when all indigenous peoples became birthright citizens.

Native Americans had special status in the United States as indigenous peoples, but immigrants had no such status. Perhaps the most important court decision bestowing birthright citizenship on immigrants under the Fourteenth Amendment was the case of the *United States v. Wong Kim Ark* in 1898. It is a precedent that still has standing today.

Wong Kim Ark: Birthright Citizenship for All

During the 1870s and 1880s, as Chinese laborers flocked to the United States to work on the railroads and in the mines, they faced much discrimination and persecution as nonwhites. Indeed, the first US anti-immigration law was passed in 1882 to prohibit further immigration by Chinese people and make them ineligible to become naturalized citizens; that is, citizens by right of meeting specific requirements. The Chinese Exclusion Acts made it legal to deny entrance into the United States to any Chinese person, even one who had previously lived in the country. In this prejudiced atmosphere, the case of Wong Kim Ark came before the US Supreme Court.

Wong Kim Ark was born in San Francisco in 1873, the child of Chinese immigrants. Although his parents were not naturalized US citizens and remained Chinese citizens, they lived and worked in America for twenty years, until they decided to return to China when Kim Ark was nine years old. The boy remained in China with his parents until 1890, when he returned to California as a teenager and found work as a cook. When he was twenty-one years old, the young man returned to China for an extended visit with his parents. Upon his return to the United States, he was denied entrance on the grounds that he was not a citizen. The man was confined to a steamship in San Francisco harbor and threatened with deportation, despite his insistence that he was an American citizen by birth. Thomas D. Riordan, a lawyer for the local Chinese aid society, took Wong's case to court, arguing that the Fourteenth Amendment guaranteed his client birthright citizenship. For months, Wong waited on ships in the harbor, not know-

Although large numbers of Chinese laborers built the US railroads in the 1800s, they were the targets of an anti-immigration law that prohibited further immigration and made them ineligible to become naturalized citizens.

ing whether he would ever see home again, while his case made its way to the US Supreme Court. Finally, on March 28, 1898, the high court ruled 6–2 in Wong's favor: he was an American citizen by right of birth.

In writing the majority opinion, Justice Horace Gray referred to the dissenting opinion of Justice Benjamin Curtis in the *Dred Scott* decision. Curtis had argued that since the words "natural born citizen" appear in the Constitution, it assumes that citizenship may be acquired at birth. The Fourteenth Amendment clarified that assumption and, wrote Gray, included "subject to the jurisdiction thereof" only for children of Indian tribes, diplomats, and enemy soldiers. While it was true, he said, that Chinese immigrants could not be naturalized and become citizens because of the current laws, this would not change the meaning of the Fourteenth Amendment. Gray wrote, "Citizenship by naturalization can only be acquired by naturalization under the authority and in the forms of law. But citizenship by birth is established by the mere fact of birth under the circumstances defined in the Constitution. Every person born in the United States, and subject to the jurisdiction thereof, becomes at once a citizen of the United States, and needs no naturalization." He thus concluded that "the American citizenship which Wong Kim Ark acquired by birth within the United States has not been lost or taken away by anything happening since his birth."[25] The Chinese Exclusion Acts could not change the fact of Wong's birthright citizenship.

The Courts Continue to Confirm Birthright Citizenship

The *Wong Kim Ark* decision became such an important precedent that the birthright citizenship question has never been successfully challenged in the courts. In 1942, for example, a group of citizens in California attempted to reverse the *Wong Kim Ark* decision and strip Japanese American citizens of their voting rights and citizenship. This occurred during World War II, when the United States was at war with Japan and anti-Japanese sentiment was strong. Many Japanese Americans were being forcibly removed from their homes and sent to internment camps in rural areas of the western states out of fear that they would be loyal to Japan and would undermine the US war effort. John T. Regan, the head of a group called Native Sons of the Golden West, sued Cameron King, the registrar of voters for San Francisco, in federal court to stop Japanese Americans from voting. The lawyer for the Native Sons argued that the *Wong Kim Ark* decision was "one of the most injurious and unfortunate decisions"[26] ever made by the Supreme Court and that Japanese Americans should not be allowed to remain citizens. He claimed that the Fourteenth Amendment was only supposed to apply to Caucasians and African Americans.

Judge Adolphus F. St. Sure was unmoved by the lawyer's argument and dismissed the case, saying that he could not change the *Wong Kim Ark* decision. The Native Sons appealed his decision to the federal Ninth Circuit Court. Again, the lawyer argued that the Wong Kim Ark decision was wrong and that the Fourteenth Amendment did not apply to minority groups. This time, the seven judges, led by Judge Curtis Wilbur, did not even bother to listen to the Japanese lawyer's side of the case. They did not even leave the courtroom in order to deliberate. They did not need to. After a quick, whispered conference, they dismissed the appeal because they believed Judge St. Sure's ruling had been correct. In the case of *Wong Kim Ark*, the US Supreme Court established birthright citizenship under the Fourteenth Amendment, and no lower court could change that fact. People born in the United States were American citizens by right of birth.

"Equal Protection"

The Supreme Court first ruled on the meaning of the Fourteenth Amendment in 1872. At issue was the phrase "equal protection of the laws" as it applies to all citizens. The state of Louisiana had passed a law limiting slaughterhouse operations to one business in a specific part of the city of New Orleans. It was forbidden to slaughter animals in other parts of the city. A group of butchers sued, claiming that their right to equal protection under the law—specifically their right to practice their trade—was abridged and that this was in violation of the Fourteenth Amendment. The case proceeded to the US Supreme Court, which ruled against the butchers. The ruling determined that the Fourteenth Amendment was meant only to apply to former slaves. It did not guarantee equal economic privileges to all citizens, no matter what their race. One dissenting justice, Stephen Johnson Field, disagreed. He thought that the Fourteenth Amendment should not be understood simply as a way to protect former slaves. Field's view would eventually prevail, and his broader interpretation would become widely accepted after the 1898 ruling in the *Wong Kim Ark* birthright citizenship case.

The Current Interpretation Debate

In modern times, John C. Eastman has been one of several legal experts who believe the Supreme Court should revisit the *Wong Kim Ark* decision because they believe that it only applies to the children of legal residents. In 1898, there was no such thing as illegal immigration, and there were no laws governing who might enter the country and settle permanently. Indeed, in his opinion affirming Wong's citizenship, Justice Gray had referred to the status of Wong's parents. He wrote,

> A child born in the United States, of parents of Chinese descent, who, at the time of his birth, are subjects of the Emperor of China, but have a permanent domicil (sic) and residence in the United States, and are there carrying on business, and are not employed in any diplomatic or official capacity under the Emperor of China, becomes at the time of his birth a citizen of the United States, by virtue of the first clause of the Fourteenth Amendment of the Constitution.[27]

In 2015, Eastman testified before Congress on immigration and border security, pointing out that Gray's decision refers specifically to the children of parents living and working permanently in the United States. He explained that the Supreme Court's ruling "in the 1898 Wong Kim Ark case is limited to lawful, permanent residents; its broader [statements that anyone born in the United States is a citizen] is erroneous and has never been adopted by the Court."[28] He insisted that the *Wong Kim Ark* decision does not apply to children of people entering the country illegally and without permission.

Eastman's point of view is, however, disputed by other legal scholars. Michael C. Dorf of Cornell University, for instance, insists that "subject to the juris-

"The 1898 Wong Kim Ark case is limited to lawful, permanent residents; its broader [statements that anyone born in the United States is a citizen] is erroneous and has never been adopted by the Court."[28]

—John C. Eastman, law professor

A border patrol agent gathers information from a group of undocumented immigrants in Texas's Rio Grande valley. Legal experts debate whether birthright citizenship applies to undocumented immigrants.

diction thereof" in the Fourteenth Amendment applies to undocumented immigrants, who must follow American law. He explains that "although *Wong Kim Ark* did not involve *undocumented* immigrant parents, its logic very much extends to them. Children born to undocumented immigrants (and for that matter, the parents themselves) are certainly subject to US jurisdiction. . . . Persons born in the US to undocumented immigrant parents are US citizens, full stop. Neither an act of Congress nor an executive order can change that. Only a constitutional amendment can."[29]

Birthright Citizenship Stands

The debate on interpreting the Fourteenth Amendment continues because the Supreme Court has never ruled precisely on whether the amendment applies to children of temporary visitors or undocumented, or illegal, immigrants. Instead, the ruling in the *Wong Kim Ark* decision has been accepted and remains the law and policy of the United States today. Birthright citizenship is granted to all who are born on American soil, no matter what the circumstances.

Chapter Three

A Magnet for Undocumented Immigrants?

Today, the *Wong Kim Ark* ruling and the broad definition of birthright citizenship remain in force. Even when people are in the country illegally, any children born to them on American soil are US citizens. Jus soli is the policy of the United States, practically speaking, and all such children have all the rights and privileges of citizens. To many people who are concerned about illegal immigration, this is a problem needing a solution. These people believe that birthright citizenship is one of the root causes of illegal immigration, enticing immigrants to enter the country illegally so that their children will be born as US citizens. Therefore, these people believe the policy needs to be revisited and revised.

Unauthorized Immigrants and Their Children

Undocumented immigration is a significant issue in the United States. The US Department of Homeland Security (DHS) defines the unauthorized resident immigrant population "as all foreign-born non-citizens who are not legal residents."[30] In a report published in 2018, the DHS estimated the unauthorized immigration population living in the United States to be 12 million as of 2015 (using the latest data then available). Other estimates of the illegal immigrant population vary widely because no one knows for sure what the actual numbers are. The Center for Migration Studies (a nonprofit educational institute) puts the number at 10.8 million. A 2018 mathematical estimate from professors at Yale University and the Massachusetts Institute of Technology suggested that 22.1 million undocumented immigrants lived in the United States. Whatever the actual number, many of these undocumented residents have children who were born in the United States.

According to the nonpartisan Migration Policy Institute, about 4 million unauthorized immigrants lived with at least one child under the age of eighteen during the period from 2012 to 2016 (the latest information available). A Pew Research Center study reports that some 250,000 babies were born to undocumented parents in 2016, equal to about 6 percent of the total number of babies born that year in the United States. Such children are sometimes pejoratively referred to as "anchor babies" because, when they are adults, they will be able to provide a path to permanent residency for their parents and other relatives. As citizens, they can

Opponents of birthright citizenship believe that it is a magnet for illegal immigration. They do not believe babies born to undocumented immigrants should have all the rights and privileges of US citizenship.

"anchor" the whole family to America. This is possible because of the 1965 Immigration and Naturalization Act, which established an immigrant preference system based on family relationships and prioritizing people with a relative who is a US citizen.

"Anchor Babies" as an Incentive for Illegal Immigration?

In today's debates over immigration policy, some Americans believe birthright citizenship is an incentive that encourages foreigners to enter the United States illegally. As long ago as 2006, Texas representative Ron Paul argued this point by saying,

> Make no mistake, Americans are happy to welcome immigrants who follow our immigration laws and see a better life here. America is far more welcoming and tolerant of newcomers than virtually any nation on earth. But our modern welfare state creates pervasive incentives for immigrants, incentives that cloud the issue of why people chose to come here. We cannot afford to open our pocketbooks to the rest of the world. We must end the pervasive incentives that encourage immigrants to come here illegally, including the anchor baby incentive.[31]

Echoing Representative Paul in 2018, South Carolina senator Lindsey Graham tweeted, "I've always supported comprehensive immigration reform—and at the same time—the elimination of birthright citizenship," adding that it "is a magnet for illegal immigration," which "needs to come to an end."[32] Several other senators, including David Vitter of Louisiana, have agreed with Graham, insisting that the financial, social, and welfare benefits of having a US citizen baby encourage women, particularly from Mexico and Central America, to enter the country illegally at the southern border.

"I've always supported comprehensive immigration reform—and at the same time—the elimination of birthright citizenship."[32]

—Senator Lindsey Graham of South Carolina

Joe Guzzardi, a writer and analyst with the organization Progressives for Immigration Reform, sums up the situation:

> Birthright citizenship is a huge magnet for illegal immigration. As a U.S. citizen, a child qualifies for affirmative benefits, free K–12 education, and more affordable in-state college tuition fees. When the child turns 21, he or she can petition for other family members to join him or her in the U.S. And thus begins the chain migration process that adds approximately four additional residents per each original immigrant.[33]

Guzzardi suggests that birthright citizenship for a child creates a path for other family members to gain citizenship without going through the rather lengthy process of legal immigration.

Refuting Some Welfare Myths

Logically, given the benefits of being a US citizen, it may seem obvious that birthright citizenship is a magnet for illegal immigration, but actual evidence that birthright citizenship is a major driver of illegal entry into the United States is difficult to find. Writing for the O'Neill Institute of Georgetown University, Sonia Canzater, a lawyer and author, argues that complaints about birthright citizenship being a magnet for illegal immigration are not based on facts. She calls this idea the "'anchor baby' myth."[34] She says that having citizen babies does nothing to protect the babies' families from deportation or to enable them to acquire permanent residency status. Canzater explains that some immigrants may believe that having an American baby will stop them from being sent back to their own country, but many unauthorized people are deported, without regard to the status of their children. US citizen children may be left in the United States with other relatives, put into the foster care system, or returned to the home country with their parents, but they do not "anchor" their parents to the United States. Canzater continues,

So, am I telling you that having a citizen child cannot garner parents U.S. citizenship? No. A citizen child is able to sponsor her parents to get green cards . . . once she turns 21 years old. Even at that time, the parents need to meet very specific character criteria in order to qualify for lawful permanent resident status. This is hardly the speedy, jump-to-the-head-of-the-line strategy described in the rhetoric of those who want to limit or revoke [the] birthright status of the children of illegal immigrants. In fact, those in law and politics know that birthright citizenship serves no immediate benefit to illegal immigrant parents.[35]

It is also untrue that undocumented immigrants can receive welfare benefits such as Medicaid or food stamps (Supplemental Nutrition Assistance Program benefits) or any other government benefits, as Paul and Vitter imply. A US citizen baby can receive Medicaid and some food assistance, but the rest of the family does not qualify. Even legal immigrants do not qualify for public assistance programs unless they have lived in the United States for at least five years. The child does have access to a free public education. In a so-called "mixed family," with perhaps one legal and one illegal parent, everyone may benefit from housing assistance, but having a citizen baby does not confer all the privileges and benefits of citizenship to a family of undocumented immigrants.

> "Those in law and politics know that birthright citizenship serves no immediate benefit to illegal immigrant parents."[35]
>
> —Sonia Canzater, lawyer

A Stressful Family Dynamic

The actual living situation for unauthorized immigrant parents with citizen children is complicated and often difficult for all involved. A young man named Bati, for example, explains how fearful his family is, despite having a citizen child. Both of Bati's parents are undocumented immigrants from Mongolia. Bati was brought to the United States by his parents when he was ten years old. His younger brother was born in America. Bati, who is twenty-one years old, is legally allowed to stay in the country because of former president Barack Obama's Deferred Action for Childhood Arrivals (DACA) policy, which continues to allow people brought to the United States as young children to remain in the country. Bati's eleven-year-old brother is an American citizen by birth. Their parents, however, know that they have no legal status and are fearful of being deported. Bati says, "They're afraid of going to the hospital and afraid of the police stopping them. If they're deported, it'll be me and my brother. Why would somebody who comes into this country have a kid just to become a citizen in 21 years and even then *wait ten years* to become a citizen? That argument doesn't really make sense. People come to the country to start a family. There's no external motive."[36]

The Benefits of Citizenship

Journalist Natasha Frost has compiled a list of the benefits of US citizenship in which she includes the following:

- Consular protection overseas kicks in whenever an American is arrested or detained abroad, with officials providing resources and aid wherever they can.
- The ability to sponsor your relatives abroad for visas or even permanent-resident green cards, eventually permitting whole families to move to the United States.
- The right to live and work in the United States, without restriction or fear of deportation. Citizens can leave for as long as they want to, without losing this right, unlike green card holders.
- Any children born overseas to two Americans are also automatically US citizens at birth. . . .
- The right to all local, federal and state benefits. Green-card holders can access some of these, including Medicare, disaster relief and healthcare programs. Only citizens get access to the full array.
- Unrestricted travel as a tourist to 177 different countries without a visa. . . .
- The right to represent the US at the Olympics. . . .
- The right to vote in federal-office elections—and arguably to choose who gets the most important job in the world. . . .
- The right to run for public office, providing you've met certain position-dependent age and time requirements. . . .
- The right to work for the federal government.

Natasha Frost, "What US Citizenship Actually Gets You: The Good and the Bad," Quartz, October 30, 2018. https://qz.com.

Bati knows that his brother's status does not protect his parents from deportation. Most undocumented immigrant parents know this as well. Guadalupe Garcia de Rayos, for example, was a thirty-five-year-old mother of two US-born children when she was deported in 2017. She had come to the United States illegally from Mexico as a teenager during the mid-1990s. She stayed in the United States, living in Arizona, and acquired a fake

Social Security number so that she could work. In 2008, she was arrested for using that number and was convicted of felony criminal impersonation in 2009. At that point, immigration authorities sought her deportation because she had been convicted of a crime. Rayos fought the deportation order. Her case and appeals went through the legal process, but by 2017, her time had run out. US Immigration and Customs Enforcement (ICE) detained her, took her to a border crossing in Nogales, Arizona, and turned her over to Mexican authorities. An ICE statement about her situation reads, "[Her] immigration case underwent review at multiple levels of the immigration court system, including the Board of Immigration Appeals, and the judges held she did not have a legal basis to remain in the US."[37]

Rayos had no choice but to remain in Mexico, and her children voluntarily went to Mexico to be with their mother. She has not given up on her desire to return to living in the United States, however. She does not think she is a criminal or that her actions warranted deportation, but she never assumed she was safe because of her children's citizenship. She explains, "The truth is I was [in the United States] for my children. For a better future. To work for them. And I don't regret it, because I did it for love. I'm going to keep fighting so that they continue to study in their country, and so that their dreams become a reality."[38]

Proud to Be an "Anchor Baby"

Even though having citizen children does not guarantee that parents can stay in the United States, sometimes such children do end up anchoring their parents to America. This is the case for Norma Juarez, who says, "I am a proud 'anchor baby,' a U.S. citizen born to undocumented parents from Mexico. Anchor babies are often perceived as children whose only purpose is to provide an undocumented parent with a 'fast track' to citizenship: thus, it is often seen as a stigma. But I embrace the label as a way of showing that I am not ashamed of my parents' undocumented status, their journey, or the life choices I had to make because of my family's circumstances."[39]

When Juarez's parents illegally crossed the border from Mexico into the United States, her mother was pregnant with Norma. The family migrated to New York, where Norma, a US citizen by birth, grew up. As a child, she witnessed her parents' anxiety and fears about having no legal status. They could not visit the child's grandparents in Mexico, for instance, because without a legal resident's green card, they would be stopped at the border and not allowed back into America. Every summer then, Norma, as the only family member for whom it was safe to do so, visited her grandparents alone. As the child grew older, her parents often joked with her that the only way they would ever get legal status was through her. They told her, "Let us wait until you are 21, maybe we will have papers then!"[40] That longed-for outcome did eventually come to pass, but the young woman struggled.

Juarez could not get financial aid for college because her parents could not risk filling out forms about their income. She tried working and going to school but eventually had to drop out. She began working for a nonprofit social service organization and became an immigration rights activist. Finally, in 2010, she was in a position to sponsor her mother to get a green card. Several months later, she was able to do the same for her father. After five years, both parents were sworn in as US citizens. Juarez returned to and graduated from college. For this one family, the American dream has become a reality, and Juarez is proud of that success and wants to help other immigrants become US citizens.

Is That Why They Came?

Juarez's story is not common. Her parents were fortunate in the end to have an "anchor baby," but that does not mean that the opportunity to have an American-born baby encourages illegal immigration. The evidence does not seem to suggest that most people who come to the United States unlawfully do so just to have an "anchor baby." Lauren Weber, a midwife in San Diego, California, estimates that only about one-third to one-quarter of her Mexican patients come to the United States specifically to have a baby. She reports, "There are a million hardworking Hispanic people in San Diego who came here to work and then happened to have a baby."[41] According to a Pew Research Center study, 90 percent of the babies born to undocumented mothers were born more than two years after the women entered the United States. This seems too long a time for having a citizen baby to be the principal reason for entering the country illegally.

Some people in parts of El Salvador (pictured) and other countries in Central America come to the United States for economic opportunities that are not available in their home countries.

Surveys conducted among unauthorized immigrants have determined that the opportunity to have a US citizen baby is rarely mentioned as a reason for their entering the United States. Crime and violence are often stated as being a major reason to leave home countries and attempt to enter the United States. Economic opportunity that is unavailable in home countries is another major factor cited by illegal immigrants. Sometimes, people come to join family already in the United States or in an effort to find a better life for their children. These responses suggest that the reasons for illegal immigration are many but usually do not include a desire to give birth to a citizen baby.

To Give Birth in America

Birthright citizenship for one's baby may not be a typical reason to enter the United States illegally, but it does happen. In 2018, Maryury Elizabeth Serrano-Hernandez; her husband, Miguel Ortiz; and their three-year-old son joined a migrant caravan from Honduras to the United States. Serrano-Hernandez was seven months pregnant. When they arrived at the US-Mexico border, the family scaled a border wall and entered the country illegally. They were picked up by border patrol agents and immediately claimed asylum. As they were being taken to a detention center, the mother began complaining of abdominal pains. She was taken to a hospital, where she gave birth to a son within a few hours. In an interview with Univision, Serrano-Hernandez called her delivery on US soil a "big reward" and remarked, "With the faith in God, I always said my son will be born [in America]." A few days later, the family members were released by immigration authorities on their own recognizance, meaning that they are trusted to show up when their asylum claim comes to court. Whether they will be granted asylum and allowed to remain legally in the United States is unknown, but the family has succeeded in having a US citizen baby.

Quoted in Barnini Chakraborty, "Honduran Woman, 19, in Migrant Caravan Scales Border Wall to Give Birth in US After 2,000-Mile Trip," Fox News, December 6, 2018. www.foxnews.com.

An Impractical Means of Acquiring Citizenship

Opinion writer and attorney Andy J. Semotiuk sums up the issue: "Although the number of illegal aliens having children in the United States has been rising over the years, the immigration benefits of having a child born in the United States are limited. Citizen children cannot sponsor parents for entry into the country until they are 21 years of age nor block their deportation by being related to the unlawfully present parent. What is more, there is a 10 year bar to re-entry if the parent has ever been in the country illegally for more than a year, which makes the notion of birthright impractical as a means of gaining immediate legal status in the USA."[42] It is therefore unlikely that birthright citizenship is a magnet for unauthorized immigration.

Chapter Four

Birth Tourism

Solid evidence that "anchor babies" are a driving force behind unauthorized immigration has not been found, but birthright citizenship does drive the phenomenon known as birth tourism. Birth tourism is the practice of visiting another country for the sole purpose of giving birth there and having a child who then obtains citizenship through birthright citizenship.

In "Little Moscow"

Sunny Isles Beach, a city just a little north of Miami, Florida, has earned the nickname of "Little Moscow." Here, hundreds of well-to-do pregnant Russian women visit every year in order to give birth in America. They come for the beautiful, warm weather; for the good medical care; for a relaxing vacation; and to give birth to a baby who will be a US citizen. Olga Zemlyanaya, for example, arrived in Florida on a tourist visa. She had no plans to remain in the country, but she did want to give birth in America and had $30,000 to make that possible, including living expenses and paying all the medical costs for her hospital stay.

In December 2018, Zemlyanaya gave birth to a daughter, and she greatly enjoyed her two-night hospital stay. In a Russian birth clinic, she would have received only basic medical care provided by a largely indifferent staff. In the Florida hospital, the nurse treated her kindly, made her feel like she was staying in a luxury hotel instead of a hospital, and gave her a menu from which to choose her meals. Zemlyanaya remembers, "And then when she said they had chocolate cake for dessert, I realized I was in paradise." Once she left the hospital, the new mother remained in Little Moscow, waiting for her baby's US passport to be processed. With the passport, mother and baby could return to Russia, secure in the knowledge that the child has a permanent place in America. Zemlyanaya explains, "With $30,000, we would not be able to buy an apartment for our child or do anything, really. But we could give her freedom. That's actually really cool."[43]

Citizen Babies from Around the World

Zemlyanaya is far from the only birth tourist to come to America in order to get a US passport for her newborn, and Russia is not the only country from which birth tourists arrive. Birth tourists do not travel to the United States as immigrants and have no intention of remaining in the country. They come for the perceived future benefits of having a citizen child, an objective made possible by the policy of birthright citizenship. In some countries, birth tourism has become extremely popular and is enthusiastically embraced by the wealthy.

No one knows how many babies are born to visiting foreign women in the United States every year or from which countries they come. No agency keeps track of this information. In 2019, the Center for Immigration Studies (CIS) estimated the number to be thirty-six thousand per year. In general, different nationalities choose different US destinations. While Russian women often opt for Florida, the preferred destination for women from China is Los Angeles. Birth tourists, however, may choose any destination city they consider appealing. For instance, in 2019, investigative reporters in Chicago probed birth tourism in their area and interviewed local obstetricians. The reporters discovered that the obstetricians "have patients who come here from other countries and pay out of pocket to deliver their babies in the United States."[44]

Most birth tourists are relatively wealthy, but others are middle-class women who have saved for years to pay for the trip. Birth

A Miami area physician performs an ultrasound exam on a Russian woman who traveled to the United States to give birth in 2019. She is one of many wealthy women from Russia who want their babies to have the privileges of US citizenship.

tourism can be expensive. Generally, the women need to visit the United States when they are about five months pregnant, because many airlines have restrictions on travel during the last few weeks of pregnancy for safety reasons. Then, after giving birth, the women need to remain in the country for the weeks it takes to finish the paperwork for the US citizen infants and acquire their passports. Hotels, apartments, hospitals, and living expenses must be covered by the tourist. With enough money, all these needs can be met comfortably, and the arrangements can be made through birth tourism packages offered in the women's home countries and in the United States.

The Business of Birth Tourism

Hundreds of enterprises specialize in bringing women to the United States to give birth, and birth tourism has become a profitable business. One such company, Miami Mama, caters primarily to Russian women and has been offering tourist packages for them since 2009. Today, say Miami Mama owners Irina and Konstantin

Lubnevskiy, the company brings about a hundred women per year to Florida to give birth to American babies. The company organizes everything for the mothers, including providing them with Russian interpreters, arranging for an apartment or hotel, scheduling medical care, applying for visas, and acquiring the newborn's citizenship documents. Miami Mama's clients may pay up to $50,000 for these services. The cost depends on the luxuriousness of the accommodations and the completeness of the assistance.

The Lubnevskiys also ensure that their clients acquire US tourist visas legally and honestly because lying on a visa application might leave the mothers open to criminal charges. They can never deny that they are pregnant and must admit that they will be giving birth in the United States. Konstantin Lubnevskiy says, "We tell every client, 'You have to tell the truth. This is America. They like the truth here.'"[45] The women who are guided through the birth tourism process by Miami Mama have no trouble going home to Russia with an American baby.

A Completely Legal Service

As long as people do not lie on their visa applications or other paperwork, birth tourism is completely legal. US Customs and Border Protection says that no laws exist regarding pregnant foreigners entering the country or giving birth on American soil. The agency explains, however, that "if a pregnant woman or anyone else uses fraud or deception to obtain a visa or gain admission to the United States, that would constitute a criminal act."[46] This means that women cannot try to conceal their pregnancies or deny them on visa applications or to customs officials as they enter the country. If asked, they have to admit that they plan to give birth in the United States but are planning to return home once the baby is born. They have to be able to demonstrate that they have the financial means to pay for medical care in America and that they will return home before the tourist visa expires. Traveling to the United States for medical care is a valid, legal reason to apply for the visa.

Taking advantage of US birthright citizenship policies and medical tourist visas in order to have an American citizen baby may seem unfair, but birth tourists and the companies that facilitate the practice do not see anything wrong with it. They say that it costs the US taxpayers nothing, that the tourists spend money that helps the US economy, and that the visitors are only seeking to have a good birthing experience and to protect their children's futures. Russell Rapoza, a physician in Fountain Valley, California, agrees. He and his colleague Chloe Zhao provide medical care to birth tourists from China. Rapoza says that 60 to 70 percent of his patients are women from China. The doctors are paid their fees in cash, as is the hospital where the women deliver, and the women and babies receive medical care that is far superior to the care available in China. Rapoza believes that complaints about birth tourism are unfounded. He explains, "Our clients are paying for everything. Not only that, but they're boosting our economy in other ways when they come here and stay. They're seeing our tourist sites. They're shopping at our stores. They're boosting our economy. I think [the criticism is] complete nonsense. I think it's only xenophobia [fear of foreigners], and really without any economic eye to it at all."[47]

Zhao, who is originally from China and now works as Rapoza's medical assistant, points out that there are distinct advantages to having a baby in the United States. She understands the reasons that women prefer to give birth in the United States rather than in China. The "painless labor" available because of the epidural (spinal) anesthesia offered in America is appealing to women in labor. In addition, she explains, "each pregnant woman has a separate room, affording patients more privacy. American doctors are not as busy as doctors in China and therefore have more patience. American doctors are principled, they encourage

> "Our clients are paying for everything. Not only that, but they're boosting our economy in other ways when they come here and stay. They're seeing our tourist sites. They're shopping at our stores."[47]
>
> —Dr. Russell Rapoza, California physician

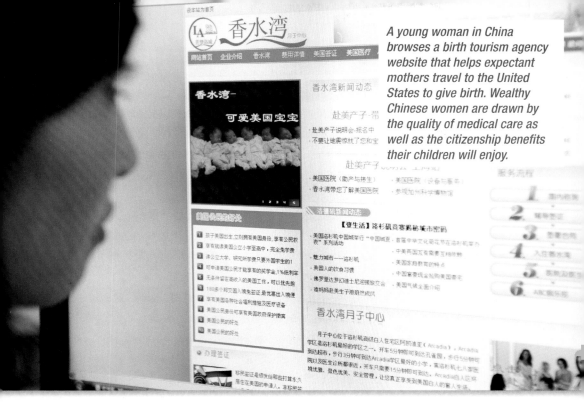

A young woman in China browses a birth tourism agency website that helps expectant mothers travel to the United States to give birth. Wealthy Chinese women are drawn by the quality of medical care as well as the citizenship benefits their children will enjoy.

patients to have natural labor [as opposed to caesarean section]. The mothers also want to give their children American citizenship."[48]

The Prize of US Citizenship

American citizenship may be a major reason that birth tourists come to the United States, but the women themselves believe that they are legally and honestly utilizing a system that benefits their children while doing no harm to anyone. Although birth tourists might select countries other than the United States for superior medical care, one Chinese birth tourism company reports that 80 percent of its clients choose America. (The other 20 percent opt for Canada.) Another company owner's clients choose the United States 100 percent of the time. Harper Hsuan, for instance, came to the United States to give birth in 2017. She insists that she did not cost American taxpayers anything and does not think the American people should object to birth tourism. She explains, "Not everyone who went to give birth in the U.S. wants to take advantage of the welfare in the U.S. If this can bring benefits to your people, why turn down the opportunity?" She does not want to use her child's birthright citizenship to immigrate to the United States herself. Her goal is to give her son the best possible future. She says of America, "It is an open and free country, and its higher education is the best in the world."[49] Someday she wants her son to have the right to attend an American university and to remain in the United States if he so chooses.

Birth tourists value American citizenship. One Russian father, Ilya Zhegulev, for example, talks about the safety of having a US passport. He worries that his home country will become too re-

---

Birth Tourism in Canada

Canada is the only other developed country in the world besides the United States that has unrestricted birthright citizenship. That situation, however, may soon change, as many Canadian citizens and government officials are debating the wisdom of the policy. In Canada, the issue is not so much undocumented immigration as it is birth tourism. Most of the birth tourists are from China, but increasing numbers come from eastern Europe or Africa. They are wealthy individuals who stay at birth hotels, give birth to a baby, and then return home with Canadian citizenship for their child. Many Canadians believe that this puts Canadian citizenship up for sale, and both liberal and conservative lawmakers are considering tightening citizenship policies. An estimated 60 percent of citizens support the idea. One lawmaker, Joe Peschisolido, argues, "It's an abuse of the system. It's a business where people are making money off of the goodness of Canadians."

Kerry Starchuk, a citizen activist fighting to restrict birth tourism, says, "It's the unfairness of it. Citizenship is not partisan, Liberal or Conservative, but about Canadian values. When you're an immigrant, you take and you contribute. [The current system] is a free-for-all." She and many others say their efforts to restrict birth tourism are about what it means to be a Canadian and maintaining a healthy community. The Canadian government was still considering changing birthright citizenship laws as of 2019.

Quoted in Sara Miller Llana, "When Does Birthright Citizenship Become Citizenship for Sale?," *Christian Science Monitor*, May 8, 2019. www.csmonitor.com.

strictive in its rules about Russians even being able to leave their country. He is especially concerned about the growing tensions between the United States and Russia. He says, "Seeing the conflict growing makes people want to take precautions because [Russia] might well close its borders. And if that happens, one would at least have a passport of a different country and be able to leave."[50]

Donny is a Chinese father who emphasizes US citizenship as the way to get the best education for his new American-born son. In Shanghai, where Donny and his wife live, entrance to the best international schools requires a foreign passport. In addition, Chinese people are registered in their hometowns no matter where they actually live, and their children must be registered there, too. Donny is not registered in Shanghai, so his child would have trouble attending schools there. He explains, "If my wife gave birth to the baby in Shanghai, there would be problems with his education. So why shouldn't I be braver and give the baby American or foreign citizenship? . . . As Chinese parents, we are slaves to our child. We want to sacrifice everything for him."[51]

Donny and his wife did not use a birth tourism company to organize their trip to the United States. As many birth tourists do, Donny made the arrangements for himself and his wife. The couple did not know that it was legal to come to the country in order to give birth, and they did not list the real reason they were visiting the United States on their visa applications. Donny remembers, "Honestly, we lied. We told them we went there as tourists. When we walked through immigration [at Los Angeles International Airport], we were really nervous. I bought my wife a long scarf to hide her belly."[52] The parents' subterfuge succeeded, however, and they returned to China with an American citizen son, but their dishonesty is considered fraud by US immigration authorities.

"If my wife gave birth to the baby in Shanghai, there would be problems with his education. So why shouldn't I be braver and give the baby American or foreign citizenship?"[51]

—Donny, Chinese birth tourist father

Deception and Fraud

Individuals making their own arrangements to go to America to give birth are not the only ones who may commit fraud in order to enter the country. Although many legitimate companies offer birth tourism packages, some companies routinely help their clients lie and circumvent American law. Thus, birth tourism is not always harmless.

In early 2019, US authorities indicted twenty people in a first-ever crackdown on birth tourism companies. The Southern California operation sprang from an ongoing investigation that began in 2015. The individuals charged ran or participated in three birth tourism companies that operated approximately three dozen so-called maternity hotels for Chinese women coming to the United States to give birth to citizen babies. Each woman paid $50,000 for her stay. The charges included conspiracy, visa fraud, tax

Ilya Zhegulev, his wife, Katya, and their son, Ivan, pose for a photo in a snowy playground in Moscow in 2019. The couple sold two cars to finance a trip to California so that their son could be born on US soil.

A Birth Tourism Package

In the western Texas border town of El Paso, an obstetrics organization offers its services to women from around the world who want to give birth in the United States. It is called Doctores Para Ti (Doctors for You), and its website touts the benefits of giving birth in America. On its home page, the business advertises, "Our medical group provides a birth program in El Paso, Texas, for international patients who wish to receive top quality medical service and obtain U.S. Citizenship for their newborn." Prices (which are nonnegotiable) for obstetric care, hospitalization, and pediatric care for the newborn are listed. Advice about hotel or apartment availability is given, and reassurances about accomplishing the visit legally are offered. Getting through immigration and into the country, says the website, is simple if one is honest and has the financial means to pay for medical care. The website warns, "Never lie to any officer regarding your intention to give birth in the United States of America. Carry all your medical documentation and be ready to provide proof that you are able to pay your medical fees (cash or receipt if you have pre-paid your medical bills)." Doctores Para Ti requires that its patients enter the United States legally, and it is eager to welcome international patients and facilitate US births.

Doctores Para Ti website. https://doctoresparati.com.

fraud, and money laundering. US attorney Nick Hanna states, "These cases allege a wide array of criminal schemes that sought to defeat our immigration laws—laws that welcome foreign visitors so long as they are truthful about their intentions when entering the country. Statements by the operators of these birthing houses show contempt for the United States, while they were luring clients with the power and prestige of U.S. citizenship for their children."[53]

Allegedly, the operators of the birth tourism businesses coached clients to lie about the purpose of their trips on their visa applications. They were told to lie about how much money they made because most did not have enough cash for their needed medical care. They were told to wear loose clothing on the trip so that customs officials would not notice their pregnancies. Some of the women also claimed to be indigent when they delivered their babies and either paid the hospitals nothing or very little. Since some of the women or their husbands worked for the Chinese government, federal authorities also worry that these citizen babies could be a future security risk to the United States. When the citizen children reach the age of twenty-one, they will be automatically eligible to sponsor their parents for permanent residence in the United States. This could be a national security risk because these people's home governments might recruit or even force them to go to the United States to spy for their government. Mark Zito, a special agent for ICE, argues, "I see this as a grave national security concern and vulnerability. Are some of them doing it for security because the United States is more stable [than their home countries]? Absolutely. But will those governments take advantage of this? Yes, they will."[54]

> "I see [birth tourism] as a grave national security concern and vulnerability. . . . Will [some foreign] governments take advantage of this? Yes, they will."[54]
>
> —Mark Zito, ICE agent

No Easy Fixes

Despite a few federal efforts to restrict birth tourism, however, the practice continues unabated. Zito explains, "We are talking about three takedowns in L.A., when there are probably 300. . . . We are trying to quell this, but it is increasing. Other nations will start taking advantage of this."[55] Birth tourism is a practice that continues to appeal to people around the world because of US birthright citizenship laws. When it is accomplished legally, there is little federal authorities can do to prevent it.

Chapter Five

Should Birthright Citizenship Be Ended?

Sahar Khan is a US citizen who was born to southern Asian parents while her father was enrolled in a post-doctoral fellowship in Boston. When she was six months old, her parents moved to Oman, a country on the Arabian Peninsula. Although she always knew she was an American citizen, she grew up in Oman had little knowledge of the country of her birth. She imagined the United States as a virtuous and desirable country, but she has never felt connected to the idea of herself as an American. She says she has always felt more like a "global citizen."[56] Nevertheless, Khan returned to the United States to attend Stanford University when she was seventeen years old, and she felt proud to claim America as her own. Today, as the nation and President Trump talk about ending birthright citizenship, she is not so sure.

When people complain about birthright citizenship abuses and disparagingly refer to "anchor babies," she is concerned and distressed. She says she feels like an "anchorless baby." She explains, "In my eyes, America emerged as an exceptionally noble nation where jus soli ('right of the soil') reigned supreme, not jus sanguinis ('right of blood'). After all, it was the exceptional law of the soil that enabled me to call America my own. Nowadays though . . . I feel like I am being disowned."[57]

What Other Countries Have Done

Khan argues that the effort to end birthright citizenship is part of a larger effort to restrict immigration and perhaps part of an effort to void America's most basic principle of equality for all races. Others, however, who argue for placing at least some restrictions on birthright citizenship, believe that controlling who gets citizenship is essential in order to maintain a national identity, ensure shared national values, and preserve America's culture for future generations. They also assert that restrictions would reduce illegal immigration.

One method of assessing the benefits and drawbacks of US citizenship policies is to examine the practices of other countries. Many countries around the world view restrictions on birthright citizenship as part of a larger policy of controlling immigration and ensuring a common national identity. While it is true that some thirty-three countries offer jus soli, or birthright citizenship, almost all of those countries are in North and South America. Elsewhere, unconditional birthright citizenship is rare. In most countries, citizenship is based on jus sanguinis, or the right of blood, meaning whether the parents are citizens. In the United Kingdom (UK), for example, according to the British Nationality Act of 1981, a child born to at least one parent who is a British citizen becomes a British citizen. Children born to non-British parents with legal, permanent residency in the UK also become citizens at birth.

Jus sanguinis is the rule in much of Europe. In 2005, Ireland had been the last European country to confer birthright citizenship when its citizenry abolished it by referendum in response to the issue of birth tourism. According to current law, a person is Irish only when at least one parent is an Irish citizen at the time of his or her birth. Some European countries are more restrictive than others. In Luxembourg, for instance, during a 2018 election, 48 percent of its adult residents were not allowed to vote because they were not citizens. The tiny country welcomes immigrants and guest workers; it treats all noncitizens well and ensures them legal protections, but it confers citizenship only rarely. Children of noncitizen residents do not become citizens at birth unless one of their parents was also born in Luxembourg. When given a chance to expand citizenship access in a 2015 referendum, 80 percent of voters rejected the idea. According to political scientist Ryan McMaken, Luxembourg's citizens worry that relaxing jus sanguinis laws "could bring about radical changes in Luxembourg through demographic shifts. A key strategy in slowing and managing this situation—while still allowing migration—is limiting access to citizenship."[58]

Switzerland and Norway are almost as restrictive of citizenship as Luxembourg, conferring birthright citizenship only on orphans or stateless children; otherwise, the child must have one parent who is a citizen. In 2017, Switzerland passed a law

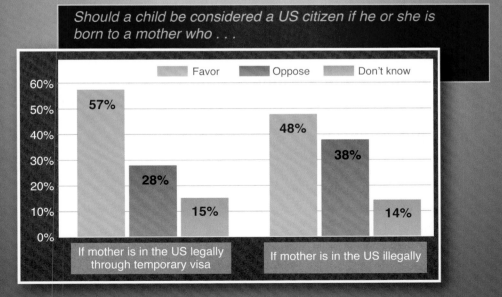

How Americans View Birthright Citizenship

Under birthright citizenship, a child born in the United States is automatically a citizen regardless of the parents' nationality. President Donald Trump has stated on more than one occasion that he wants to do away with birthright citizenship. The 2018 American Barometer survey, conducted by Hill.TV and the HarrisX polling company, reveals that Americans generally support birthright citizenship, although the level of support changes depending on the parents' legal status.

Should a child be considered a US citizen if he or she is born to a mother who . . .

Favor   Oppose   Don't know

If mother is in the US legally through temporary visa: 57%, 28%, 15%

If mother is in the US illegally: 48%, 38%, 14%

Source: Emily Ekins, "What Americans Think About Birthright Citizenship," Cato Institute, November 14, 2018. www.cato.org.

allowing citizenship for third-generation children born in Switzerland whose parents had lived in the country for at least ten years, who have attended Swiss schools for at least five years, and who have a grandparent with permanent legal residency in the country. Poland requires both parents to be citizens for a child born there to automatically become a citizen.

Birthright citizenship is also unusual outside of Europe. Japan, for example, is strictly a jus sanguinis country, excepting only orphans or stateless infants. Russia has similar laws. In Qatar and Kuwait, children become citizens at birth only if their fathers are citizens. Australia and New Zealand grant birthright citizenship only if one parent is a citizen or permanent resident of the country, although in the past both countries allowed citizenship for anyone born on their soil. Both countries changed their policies in response to birth tourism and illegal immigration problems. The last country to repeal birthright citizenship laws was the Carib-

America's Opinion

A majority of Americans have long supported birthright citizenship, despite any perceived problems. A 2011 Pew Research Center poll found that 57 percent of Americans favor leaving the Constitution as is in regard to birthright citizenship. That percentage has not changed a great deal over the years. In a 2018 survey conducted by the *Hill* and HarrisX, a thousand registered voters were asked about birthright citizenship and the legal status of the parents. Again, 57 percent of respondents approved of birthright citizenship if the mother was not a citizen but was living legally in the United States. When considering undocumented status, opinions differed between those identifying themselves as Republicans versus those self-identified as Democrats. About 62 percent of Republicans would deny citizenship status to babies born to mothers who were illegally in the country. Only 18 percent of Democrats said the same. Among Independents, 39 percent would deny citizenship status to a child born to a mother who was in the United States illegally, while 48 percent would approve the child's citizenship.

bean island nation of the Dominican Republic, in 2013, when the country became concerned about the flood of immigrants from neighboring Haiti.

Why Restrict Birthright Citizenship?

In many countries where birthright citizenship has been reversed or never existed, it is commonly believed that birthright citizenship produces a percentage of citizens who have different values and experiences than the nation's cultural majority. Some critics believe that instead of assimilating into their society and being loyal to their birth country, these immigrants might remain loyal to ancestral countries and cultures instead. It is assumed these birthright citizens and their families might eventually threaten the very nature of their adopted countries. McMaken explains, "Thus, jus sanguinis requirements became an attractive means of slowing down the process of integrating new citizens and of ensuring that new migrant groups would integrate through native parentage, marriage, or through long terms of residency."[59]

British prime minister Margaret Thatcher, in explaining why she supported the elimination of the UK's unconditional birthright citizenship, said in 1978,

> There was a committee which looked at it and said that if we went on as we are then by the end of the century there would be four million people of the new Commonwealth or Pakistan here. Now, that is an awful lot and I think it means that people are really rather afraid that this country might be rather swamped by people with a different culture and, you know, the British character has done so much for democracy, for law, and done so much throughout the world that if there is any fear that it might be swamped, people are going to react and be rather hostile to those coming in.[60]

Similar fears still impact birthright citizenship arguments four decades later. If the United States were to adopt Thatcher's position, argue many people, it would be helping preserve the national character and culture of America. These people argue that birthright citizenship should be eliminated or at least restricted in various ways. Others are more cautious.

The Case for Maintaining Birthright Citizenship

Some commentators who champion birthright citizenship point out that the United States is unique in its national character and cannot be compared with other countries. It is made up of immigrants from many countries around the world and always has been. If birthright citizenship were not the law of the land, the nation and its character might change in unintended and negative ways. Roger Clegg, president of the Center for Equal Opportunity, argues, "America has been hugely successful over the years in assimilating its immigrants and it is reasonable to assume that birthright citizenship has been part of our winning formula."[61]

Niger Innis of the Congress of Racial Equality says, "We are a nation of assimilated immigrants."[62] He points out that the problem in Europe with immigrants is that they often do not assimilate into their new countries and instead remain apart from the national culture. He and many others believe that birthright citizenship is a major reason that people from different countries assimilate successfully in America. According to the National Academy of Sciences, the results of several studies suggest that birthright citizenship "is one of the most powerful mechanisms of formal political and civic inclusion in the United States."[63]

The Example of Germany

Germany's experience with relaxing its citizenship policies may hold a powerful lesson for the United States about the benefits of birthright citizenship and successful assimilation.

"We are a nation of assimilated immigrants."[62]

—Niger Innis, National Spokesperson for the Congress of Racial Equality

Turkish shops in Germany serve a large guest worker population from Turkey. Germany opened its borders to guest workers, many of whom remained there, married, and gave birth to children who were not citizens.

Traditionally, Germany granted citizenship at birth only to those children born to German parents. From the 1950s through the 1970s, Germany opened its borders to guest workers, including about 750,000 people from Turkey. About half of those Turkish workers did not return to their home countries but remained in Germany, married, and gave birth to children who were not citizens. Today, an estimated 2.5 million Turks reside in Germany. Many are second- and third-generation residents, but they did not assimilate well into German society. In many ways, they were second-class citizens, more likely to be poor, attend low-quality schools, suffer poor health, and commit crimes. Their preferred language, society, and culture remained separate from that of the rest of Germany.

The German government considered the situation an assimilation crisis, and in 2000, it began relaxing its citizenship requirements. It passed a law making children citizens by birth if one of their parents had legally resided in Germany for at least eight years. Studies of the children granted birthright citizenship reveal some remarkable advantages over those without citizenship. Alex Nowrasteh, director of immigration studies at the Cato Institute, a libertarian think tank, reports, "Immigrant parents of children newly covered by birthright citizenship gained more German friends, spoke more German, and read German newspapers more than others. They enrolled their children in preschool at a higher rate and started them earlier in primary school, which prompted a rise in German language proficiency and a decrease in social and emotional problems."[64] German social scientists have concluded that birthright citizenship encourages assimilation for entire families and may be crucial to immigration success. Granting birthright citizenship to Turkish residents did not change the character of Germany. Instead, these residents began to see themselves as German.

Rejected and Unequal

On the other hand, when the Dominican Republic eliminated birthright citizenship for unauthorized immigrants in 2013 and made the law retroactive to 1929, an estimated two hundred thousand people of Haitian descent became stateless. These Haitians had been migrating to the Dominican Republic for decades (Haiti and the Dominican Republic share the island of Hispaniola), often working at the lowest-paying jobs that the native born did not want to do. They lived permanently in the Dominican Republic and had children there. Now, they and their descendants are noncitizens, with few rights and subject to deportation at any time. Many have never been to Haiti and know little about the country, and yet the country of their birth rejects them. Many remain in the Dominican Republic, but their status is so uncertain that children cannot enroll in schools and parents cannot obtain legal employment. Even acquiring permanent resident status is difficult and requires navigating a complicated government bureaucracy that is too burdensome for poverty-stricken Haitians to cope with. What will become of these stateless Haitians is unknown.

According to the Migration Policy Institute, a liberal Washington, DC, think tank, repealing birthright citizenship could lead to a similar undocumented stateless population in the United States of 25 million by 2050. These people would have no legal protections, no federal benefits, and no health care. They would have little incentive or ability to assimilate into the larger American society. Journalist Emily Moon points out that "citizenship—and all its attendant benefits—has long been recognized as one way to 'level the playing field' between native-born and immigrant children."[65]

Blog editor Crystal Ayres writes that birthright citizenship also prevents a society from developing rigid classes or castes

Haitians who were once considered citizens of the Dominican Republic wait to board buses back to Haiti after the Dominican government revoked citizenship laws for Haitian immigrants.

of people and ensures that everyone in
the nation is equal under the law. She
explains, "Birthright citizenship is
the ultimate form of equality. . . .
Without it, societies would begin
to form caste systems. At the top are
those who are natural citizens. In the mid-
dle are those who could afford to purchase
their citizenship. Then, at the bottom, are the immigrants who are allowed to be present, but not allowed to have the right to pursue citizenship."[66] Such an
outcome seems antithetical to American values, according
to Ayres and other critics. It would mean official, legal discrimination against whole groups of people.

> "Birthright citizenship
> is the ultimate form of
> equality."[66]
>
> —Crystal Ayres, blog editor
> and author

Do the Benefits Outweigh the Drawbacks?

Even if the benefits of maintaining birthright citizenship in the
United States are indisputable, it is also undeniable that abuses
of the policy exist. Clegg argues that the fact that abuses, such
as some birth tourists or illegal immigrants coming to the United
States in order to have citizen babies, "can occur is not enough
to scrap an approach if it makes sense in the vast majority of
circumstances."[67] He and many others insist that abolishing birthright citizenship is not justified in order to prevent abuses that
occur in a few circumstances.

Perhaps the United States has to accept those abuses as a
tiny percentage of the citizenship births that happen each year.
Or perhaps slight changes in the policy could be made to prevent
some of those outcomes. Some proposals for limiting birth tourism, for example, include increasing crackdowns on maternity
hotels, which often commit fraud and encourage mothers to lie
to immigration authorities, or perhaps denying visas to pregnant
women from countries known for birth tourism. Another proposal
is to pass a law making it illegal to enter the United States for the
purpose of giving birth. Others have suggested that a minimal

Korean in Japan

Zainichi is the Japanese term for Koreans who are residents of Japan, and there were 484,627 of them registered in Japan as of 2017. Many are third- or fourth-generation residents of the country. They are not citizens, no matter how long they have lived in Japan nor where they were born. In Japan, citizenship is based strictly on Japanese parentage. Historically, *Zainichi* have faced discrimination and lower economic status in Japan, and although their situation has improved, discrimination still exists today. Some Koreans want to integrate into and embrace the Japanese culture, while others cling to their ethnic roots and identify as primarily Korean. The *Zainichi* of today often do not have a clear identity. They are "marginalized in Japan and viewed as foreigners in Korea," according to Jang Hawon, a professor at China's Peking University who has studied their situation. Jang argues, "Japan should pay attention to Zainichi Koreans . . . for the purpose of promoting a more mature multicultural society." Noncitizen ethnic groups can have a difficult time integrating into their larger societies.

Jang Hawon, "The Special Permanent Residents in Japan: Zainichi Korean," *Yale Review of International Studies*, January 2019. http://yris.yira.org.

residency requirement for the mother would prevent the almost accidental citizenship of some children. Hiroshi Motomura, a law professor at the University of California, Los Angeles, on the other hand, recommends leaving well enough alone. He says, "There are some times the rules benefit more than the group you intended it to, but the group you intended it to benefit is significant and larger, and so you stick with the rule."[68]

An American Ideal

President Ronald Reagan once said, "An immigrant can live in France but not become a Frenchman; he can live in Germany but not become a German; he can live in Japan but not become Japanese, but anyone from any part of the world can come to America and become an American."[69] The citizens of the United States have to ask themselves whether that is an American ideal that they really want to change.

Introduction: Citizens at Birth

1. Quoted in Jonathan Swan and Stef W. Kight, "Exclusive: Trump Targeting Birthright Citizenship with Executive Order," *Axios*, October 30, 2018. www.axios.com.

2. Quoted in John Wagner, Josh Dawsey, and Felicia Sonmez, "Trump Vows Executive Order to End Birthright Citizenship, a Move Most Legal Experts Say Would Run Afoul of the Constitution," *Washington Post*, October 30, 2018. www.washingtonpost.com.

3. Quoted in Wagner et al., "Trump Vows Executive Order to End Birthright Citizenship."

4. Raul A. Reyes, "Trump's Claim of Ending Birthright Citizenship Is a Callous and Dangerous Political Stunt," *The Hill* (Washington, DC), October 31, 2018. https://thehill.com.

5. Quoted in Ted Hesson, "Can Trump Revoke Birthright Citizenship? Nearly All on Left and Right Say No," *Politico*, October 30, 2018. www.politico.com.

Chapter One: The History of Birthright Citizenship

6. Ruth Bader Ginsburg, "Remarks on Women Becoming Part of the Constitution," *Law & Inequality: A Journal of Theory and Practice*, vol. 6, no. 1, p. 17.

7. Mary Beth Norton, "The Constitutional Status of Women in 1787," *Law & Inequality: A Journal of Theory and Practice*, vol. 6, no. 1, p. 8.

8. Quoted in Amy Briggs, "How the Founding Fathers Understood Citizenship," National Geographic, October 31, 2018. www.nationalgeographic.com.

9. Quoted in John Woodman, "Evidence Found That American Common Law Defined Whether a Child Born on US Soil of Non-Citizen Parents Was a Natural Born Citizen! (*Lynch v Clarke*, 1844)," *Investigating the Obama Birth Mysteries* (blog), July 6, 2012. www.obamabirthbook.com.

10. Quoted in A. Leon Higginbotham Jr., "Chief Justice Roger Taney's Defense and Justice Thurgood Marshall's Condem-

nation of the Precept of Black Inferiority," Race, Racism, and the Law. https://racism.org.

11. Quoted in Toni Konkoly, "Famous Dissents: *Dred Scott v Sandford* (1857)," Thirteen, WNET, December 2006. www .thirteen.org.

12. Quoted in NCC Staff, "*Dred Scott* Decision Still Resonates Today," National Constitution Center, March 6, 2019. https:// constitutioncenter.org.

13. Quoted in Facing History and Ourselves, "The Civil Rights Act of 1866." www.facinghistory.org.

14. Quoted in Garrett Epps, "The Citizenship Clause Means What It Says," *Atlantic*, October 30, 2018. www.theatlantic .com.

15. Quoted in Facing History and Ourselves, "Congress Debates the Fourteenth Amendment." www.facinghistory.org.

16. Quoted in Facing History and Ourselves, "Congress Debates the Fourteenth Amendment."

17. Quoted in Facing History and Ourselves, "Congress Debates the Fourteenth Amendment."

18. Garrett Epps, "The Struggle over the Meaning of the 14th Amendment Continues," *Atlantic*, July 10, 2018. www.the atlantic.com.

Chapter Two: Interpreting the Fourteenth Amendment

19. Epps, "The Citizenship Clause Means What It Says."

20. Epps, "The Citizenship Clause Means What It Says."

21. Quoted in J. Craig Williams and Robert Ambrogi, "Birthright Citizenship and the Fourteenth Amendment," Interview Transcript, Lawyer 2 Lawyer, Legal Talk Network, November 12, 2018. https://legaltalknetwork.com.

22. Quoted in Williams and Ambrogi, "Birthright Citizenship and the Fourteenth Amendment."

23. Quoted in Williams and Ambrogi, "Birthright Citizenship and the Fourteenth Amendment."

24. Quoted in National Constitution Center Staff, "On This Day, All Indians Made United States Citizens," Constitution Daily (blog), National Constitution Center, June 2, 2019. https:// constitutioncenter.org.

25. Legal Information Institute, "*United States v. Wong Kim Ark*," Cornell Law School, Cornell University. www.law.cornell.edu.

26. Quoted in Wherever There's a Fight, "Attempt to Strip Japanese Americans of Voting Rights," 2013. www.wherever theresafight.com.
27. Quoted in Legal Information Institute, *United States v. Wong Kim Ark*."
28. Quoted in Andrew R. Arthur, "Birthright Citizenship: An Overview," Center for Immigration Studies, November 5, 2018. https://cis.org.
29. Michael C. Dorf, "Can Trump Eliminate Birthright Citizenship? Can Congress?," *Dorf on Law* (blog), October 30, 2018. www.dorfonlaw.org.

Chapter Three: A Magnet for Undocumented Immigrants?

30. US Department of Homeland Security, "Estimates of the Unauthorized Immigrant Population Residing in the United States." www.dhs.gov.
31. Quoted in Federation for Immigration Reform, "Birthright Citizenship," 2010. www.fairus.org.
32. Quoted in Steve Byas, "Lindsey Graham to Introduce Bill to Eliminate Birthright Citizenship," *New American*, October 31, 2018. www.thenewamerican.com.
33. Joe Guzzardi, "Commentary: Supreme Court Must Resolve Controversy over Birthright Citizenship," Fredericksburg.com, November 10, 2018. www.fredericksburg.com.
34. Sonia Canzater, "'Anchor Babies,' 'Birth Tourism,' and Most Americans' Complete Ignorance of Immigration Law," O'Neill Institute, Georgetown Law, January 22, 2018. http://oneill.law.georgetown.edu.
35. Canzater, "'Anchor Babies,' 'Birth Tourism,' and Most Americans' Complete Ignorance of Immigration Law."
36. Quoted in Esther Yu Hsi Lee, "These Photos Prove 'Anchor Babies' Are a Myth," Think Progress, August 28, 2015. https://thinkprogress.org.
37. Quoted in Steve Almasy, Emanuella Grinberg, and Ray Sanchez, "'I Did It for Love' Says Mother Deported in Arizona Immigration Case," CNN, February 10, 2017. www.cnn.com.
38. Quoted in Almasy et al., "'I Did It for Love' Says Mother Deported in Arizona Immigration Case."
39. Norma Juarez, "From Anchor Baby to Activist: An Immigration Story," Public Seminar.org, September 5, 2017. www.publicseminar.org.

40. Juarez, "From Anchor Baby to Activist."
41. Quoted in Louis Jacobson, "Fact-Checking the Claims About 'Anchor Babies' and Whether Illegal Immigrants 'Drop and Leave,'" PolitiFact, August 6, 2010. www.politifact.com.
42. Andy J. Semotiuk, "Born in the USA but Not American?," *Forbes*, October 30, 2018. www.forbes.com.

Chapter Four: Birth Tourism
43. Quoted in Iuliia Stashevska, "Mother Russia: South Florida Sees a Boom in 'Birth Tourism,'" AP News, March 22, 2019. www.apnews.com.
44. Chuck Goudie and Barb Markoff, "Birth Tourism Controversy: Foreign Women Travel to Deliver Babies, Gain U.S. Citizenship for Newborns," ABC7, Eyewitness News, May 22, 2019. https://abc7chicago.com.
45. Quoted in Cynthia McFadden, Sarah Fitzpatrick, Tracy Connor, and Anna Schecter, "Birth Tourism Brings Russian Baby Boom to Miami," NBC News, January 9, 2018. www.nbcnews.com.
46. Quoted in McFadden et al., "Birth Tourism Brings Russian Baby Boom to Miami."
47. Quoted in Jennifer Pak, "Providing Medical Care to 'Birth Tourists' from China," Marketplace.org, March 13, 2019. www.marketplace.org.
48. Quoted in Pak, "Providing Medical Care to 'Birth Tourists' from China."
49. Quoted in Jennifer Pak, "Why Chinese Parents Come to America to Give Birth," Marketplace.org, March 6, 2019. www.marketplace.org.
50. Quoted in Stashevska, "Mother Russia."
51. Quoted in Pak, "Why Chinese Parents Come to America to Give Birth."
52. Quoted in Pak, "Why Chinese Parents Come to America to Give Birth."
53. Quoted in Doug Stanglin, "20 Charged in California in Crackdown on 'Birth Tourism' for Expectant Mothers from China," *USA Today*, January 31, 2019. www.usatoday.com.
54. Quoted in Amy Taxin, "20 Charged in Chinese Birth Tourism Crackdown," AP News, February 1, 2019. www.apnews.com.
55. Quoted in Miriam Jordan, "3 Arrested in Crackdown on Multimillion-Dollar 'Birth Tourism' Businesses," *New York Times*, January 31, 2019. www.nytimes.com.

56. Sahar Khan, "An Anchor Baby's America," *HuffPost* (blog), March 25, 2017. www.huffpost.com.

57. Khan, "An Anchor Baby's America."

58. Ryan McMaken, "Why Birthright Citizenship Is Rare in Europe," Mises Institute, February 19, 2019. https://mises.org.

59. McMaken, "Why Birthright Citizenship Is Rare in Europe."

60. Quoted in Nolan Rappaport, "Most Countries Agree with Trump About Birthright Citizenship," *The Hill* (Washington, DC), November 8, 2018. https://thehill.com.

61. Roger Clegg, "Five Mistakes Some Conservatives Are Making on Immigration Policy," Center for Equal Opportunity. www.ceousa.org.

62. Niger Innis, "What I've Learned as a Native-Born 'Dreamer': We Are a Nation of Assimilated Immigrants," *The Hill* (Washington, DC), February 5, 2018. https://thehill.com.

63. Quoted in Alex Nowrasteh, "Birthright Citizenship Isn't Just the Law, It's Crucial to Assimilation in the U.S.," Cato Institute, November 1, 2018. www.cato.org.

64. Nowrasteh, "Birthright Citizenship Isn't Just the Law, It's Crucial to Assimilation in the U.S."

65. Emily Moon, "What Would Ending Birthright Citizenship Mean for the United States?," *Pacific Standard*, October 30, 2018. https://psmag.com.

66. Crystal Ayres, "10 Birthright Citizenship Pros and Cons," Vittana (blog). https://vittana.org.

67. Clegg, "Five Mistakes Some Conservatives Are Making on Immigration Policy."

68. Quoted in Jesusemen Oni, "Foreigners Seeking US Citizenship for Children Flout Law, Can Endanger Babies," VOA News, December 6, 2016. http://voanews.com.

69. Quoted in Alex Nowrasteh, "Birthright Citizenship: An American Idea That Works," Cato Institute, July 20, 2018. www.cato.org.

American Immigration Council—
www.americanimmigrationcouncil.org

This nonpartisan organization is working toward a fair and just American immigration system. Click "Topics" to explore its ideas about birthright citizenship.

Center for Equal Opportunity—www.ceousa.org

This conservative think tank focuses on three major issues in the areas of race and ethnicity: immigration, affirmative action, and bilingual education. Navigate to the topic labeled "Assimilation" to read articles on birthright citizenship.

Center for Immigration Studies—https://cis.org

This nonpartisan, nonprofit organization provides information about all aspects of legal and illegal immigration and its effects in the United States. It offers a large section on birthright citizenship.

Center for Migration Studies of New York—https://cmsny.org

This think tank and educational institute promotes the dignity and rights of immigrants and conducts research about immigration policy. Explore its research section to learn its conclusions on immigration reform and more.

Constitutional Accountability Center—
www.theusconstitution.org

This self-described progressive organization is a think tank, an advocacy center, and a law firm. It advocates for a liberal view of a "living" (i.e., changing with the times) Constitution. Two major issues for the group are immigration and citizenship, which include securing and protecting birthright citizenship.

Migration Policy Institute — www.migrationpolicy.org

This nonpartisan organization is devoted to research and providing reliable information about immigration issues around the world. Visitors to its website can explore topics related to integration (assimilation) of migrants, migrant children, migrants and education, and much more.

Books

Leo Chavez, *Anchor Babies and the Challenge of Birthright Citizenship*. Stanford, CA: Stanford University Press, 2017.

Cari Lee Skogberg Eastman, *Immigration: Examining the Facts*. Santa Barbara, CA: ABC-CLIO, 2017.

D.J. Herda, *Slavery and Citizenship: The* Dred Scott *Case*. New York: Enslow, 2017.

Stuart Kallen, *Crisis on the Border: Refugees and Undocumented Immigrants*. San Diego: ReferencePoint, 2019.

George Takei, Justin Eisinger, and Steven Scott, *They Called Us Enemy*. Marietta, GA: Top Shelf, 2019.

Juan Pablo Villalobos, *The Other Side: Stories of Central American Teen Refugees Who Dream of Crossing the Border*. New York: Farrar, Straus & Giroux, 2019.

Sandra Neil Wallace and Rich Wallace, *First Generation: 36 Trailblazing Immigrants and Refugees Who Make America Great*. New York: Little, Brown, 2018.

Internet Sources

Constitutional Timeline: National Constitution Center. https://constitutioncenter.org. This online exhibit is an interactive exploration of the key events in constitutional history, including the Fourteenth Amendment.

Library of Congress, "Birthright Citizenship Around the World," February 28, 2019. https://www.loc.gov. With maps and charts, the federal law library allows visitors to search for and identify citizenship and naturalization laws in the countries of the world.

ProCon.org, "Birthright Citizenship Debate: Should Children Born on US Soil to Undocumented Immigrants Automatically Have US Citizenship?" https://immigration.procon.org. Visitors to this site can read fair, balanced pro and con arguments about birthright citizenship and whether it should be restricted or maintained.

Picture Credits

Cover: Ryan Rodrick Beiler

 6: Michael Candelori/Shutterstock
10: The Signing of the Constitution of the United States in 1787, 1940 (oil on canvas), Christy, Howard Chandler (1873–1952)/ Hall of Representatives, Washington D.C., USA/Bridgeman Images
13: Poster advertising a meeting to discuss the 'Dred Scott (1799–1858) Case', 1857 (litho), American School, (19th century)/Private Collection/Peter Newark American Pictures/ Bridgeman Images
17: Hannamariah/Shutterstock
21: Associated Press
25: Charles Crocker (1822–88) and his Chinese workforce constructing the Central Pacific Railroad, completed 1869 (colour litho), American School, (19th century)/Private Collection/Peter Newark American Pictures/Bridgeman Images
29: vichinterlang/Stock
31: Vivid Pixels/Shutterstock
35: Monkey Business Images/Shutterstock
39: MCCAIG/iStock
44: Associated Press
47: Associated Press
50: Associated Press
55: Maury Aaseng
59: Associated Press
61: Associated Press

Toney Allman holds degrees from Ohio State University and the University of Hawaii. She currently lives in Virginia, where she enjoys a rural lifestyle as well as researching and writing about a variety of topics for students.